I Loved You *before* I Met You

I Loved You *before* I Met You

A Love Story in Poetry

BRAODRICK PATRICK

RESOURCE *Publications* • Eugene, Oregon

I LOVED YOU BEFORE I MET YOU
A Love Story in Poetry

Copyright © 2024 Braodrick Patrick. All rights reserved. Except for brief quotations in critical publications or reviews, no part of this book may be reproduced in any manner without prior written permission from the publisher. Write: Permissions, Wipf and Stock Publishers, 199 W. 8th Ave., Suite 3, Eugene, OR 97401.

Resource Publications
An Imprint of Wipf and Stock Publishers
199 W. 8th Ave., Suite 3
Eugene, OR 97401

www.wipfandstock.com

PAPERBACK ISBN: 979-8-3852-0830-2
HARDCOVER ISBN: 979-8-3852-0831-9
EBOOK ISBN: 979-8-3852-0832-6

02/29/24

To the root of my love.
To my greatest desire.
To the greatest gift given.

For I am nothing
without your love.

For our love is written
in the heavens amongst the stars.

WRITTEN IN THE STARS

What if I told you
that I loved you
before I met you.

What if I told you
that our love was
written in the heavens
amongst the stars.

Like comets that explodes in the nights sky,
our love is forever intertwined.

We were bonded at the sight of creation
two souls equally matched
yet so close and so far, apart.

Contents

About the Novel	xi
Introduction	xiii
Chapter One: Memories	1
Journal entry "Month of May."	1
Thy Love At First Sight	2
First Conversation	4
Journal entry "Month of May."	5
Arrival	6
A Drink From Thy Lips	7
Silently Watching	9
Conversation Of Love	10
Unspoken Words Of Love	11
Counting Stars	12
Tomorrow Is Promised	13
Chapter Two: Everlasting Love	14
Journal entry "Month of May."	14
Morning Desire	15
Everlasting Love	16
Morning Breaks	17
Journal entry "Month of May."	18
Small Thoughts	19
Journal entry "Month of May."	20

Contents

Thy Love Is Like Summer	21
Journal entry "Month of May."	22
Summertime Loving	23
Sight Of Love	24
Journal entry "Month of May."	25
Catch Me If You Dare	26
Kiss Me Into Tonight	27
Journal entry "Month of May."	28
Journal entry "Month of May."	29
Words Of Others	30
Journal entry "Month of May."	31
Counting Rose Peddles	32
Drifting Into The Night	33
Journal entry "Month of May."	34
Chapter Three: Lady Of The Sea	35
Journal entry "Month of June."	35
Deep Breaths Of Life	36
Wondering Love	37
Lady Of The Sea	38
Journal entry "Month of June."	39
A Call In The Night	41
Beyond The Night Lights Of Midnight	42
Journal entry "Month of June."	43
Forever Bound	44
Love Heals With Time	45
Morning Light	46
Thy Morning Kiss	47
Together In Love	48
Journal entry "Month of June."	49
Taste Of Love	50
Counting Days	51
Chapter Four: Forbidden Love	52
Journal entry "Month of June."	52
Dreamful Dreams	54
Loving Summer	55

Contents

Fading Love	56
Take My Love With You	57
Journal entry "Month of June."	58
Loves Reflection	59
Cloudy Dreams	60
Forbidden Love	61
Promise Me Tomorrow	62
Pictures On The Wall	63
Forever In Arms	65
Chapter Five: Time Flies	**66**
Journal entry "Month of July."	66
Broken Words	67
Shades Of Love	68
Nothing Is Forbidden	69
Journal entry "Month of August Final Entry."	70
When I'm Gone	71
Remember Me	72
Kiss From Lady Of The Night	73
Journal entry "The End."	74
Loves Core	75
About The Author	77

About the Novel

Discovering her lovers journal, a journal she promised to never read and quickly discovers that the journal is filled with his poetic thoughts regarding their love story. This book is written in a collection of poems and storytelling about two teenagers, who fall in love at first sight. But sometimes love doesn't last forever as one of them quickly discover that their cancer has return and a battle that was thought to have been beaten is far from over. Could this be the end of love at first sight or is this the beginning of a true love story, because sometimes love itself is written in the heavens amongst the stars. The novel is split into five chapters, memories, everlasting love, lady of the sea, forbidden love, and time flies.

Introduction

Dear Readers,

To understand love, we must first understand loss.

Mourning dear love and the day I open your journal. Where are you amongst the heavens of the stars, for your presence here no longer exist. Just an emptiness void that took your place.

I guess this is it. This is life without you. I saw your journal as I packed your cloths away. For you will no longer need them where you're going. I saw thy journal; owe how I promised thee never to read. Yet you are gone, and your presence no longer comforts me. Your promise for forever is now free.

Yet my heart yarns to be close to thee. I dared thyself not to read, yet the emptiness void screamed to fell something of complete. My heart, my heart, skipped a beat as my hands moved closer and opened the journal, I promise thee never to read. For I miss you and this is all that I have left of thee.

As death has come and fled with thee. So, I opened and started to read the journal I promised thee never to read, and that's when my eyes opened and my heart was able to see, the love thee had for me.

Chapter One

Memories

JOURNAL ENTRY "MONTH OF MAY."

It almost the end of the month of May when we meet, it seems as if it was yesterday that your eyes caught me looking at you. Yet if only you knew, the thoughts that were running through my mind that day, the thoughts that are written between these lines of love.

THY LOVE AT FIRST SIGHT

The bell ring and that when I say you.
When I saw you
I knew I loved you.

When I saw you
I knew that this was it.

The deep lines driven across thy lips
with only the thought of the
taste from thy kiss.
I knew I'll love you forever
I knew I'll love you even when
you couldn't love yourself.

I knew I'll love you beyond
life and death itself.

But then thy eyes
caught me looking
so, I glared away.

Yet my heart screamed
for my eyes to stay
while my ears heard
thy footsteps walk away.

The bell ringed
and that's when I knew
summer was here
and you couldn't stay.

FIRST CONVERSATION

We were only 17
but I was madly in love with thee.
I walked outside and saw you
at the bus stop and you saw me.

We stared at each other as the wind blew.
You started to walk over
God knows how I held my breath.
You gave me your name and I gave you mines.

You ask me do I party.
Owe how I stuttered at the thought
you asked me to come to the after-school party
yet my response seemed to not form shape
and that's when the bus came
and you walked away.

I whisper I love you
but the words caught silence
in its wake.

JOURNAL ENTRY "MONTH OF MAY."

I arrived home, but only the thoughts of you flood my mind. The thought that you had asked me

to come to the party tonight, although I know you are way out of my lead. But I come willingly towards your gravitational pull.

So, I guess I'll see you tonight.

ARRIVAL

The sun crawled under the moon,
as they kissed each other goodnight.

Yet only the sight of you
consumed my thoughts.
You asked me to come
and so, I did.

I saw the red cup of liquor
consume a kiss from thy lips.
Yet the music drowned me
at every sip taken from thy lips.

All I could think of was
what it would be like
to have a drink
from thy lips.

A DRINK FROM THY LIPS

What is love?
Is it not from thy lips?

One could wonder
of the taste
from thy kiss.

A drink from thy lips
is it not like a drink from true love kiss?
The deep touch of moist from thy lips
thanking God for thy kiss.

Only heaven could have made such lips.
Thy mind drowning in one's kiss
only to think of the days
thy lips were missed.

A sculpture designed from the heavens
that were placed upon thy lips.
Sweet and tenderness
yet bitter at every kissed.

Mind overly drawn in thy mist
with thy heart forever confined
in one's kiss.

Because a drink from thy lips
is like a drink from true love
kiss.

SILENTLY WATCHING

Take me away from this place.
Let me fly into the distance
of tomorrow.
Into the glimpse of the night.
Heart craving at the reflection
of your sight.

As eyes stare threw the window glass
into the distance of tonight.

Knowing at the kiss of morning
that thy love would be out of sight.

But then you walked over to me
and said hi.

CONVERSATION OF LOVE

I stared at you
and you stared at me.
we talked for hours
about nothing.
Yet we talked
about everything.

I scanned and captured
every dimple placed
upon your cheeks.
I saw you laugh at every
second of my heartbeat.

The clock stroked twelve,
then one, then two, then three.
Yet at the stroke of four,
you were headed out the door.

But then you stopped and looked back at me
as your hands started to speak.
Come,
Come walk with me.

UNSPOKEN WORDS OF LOVE

Night sky captures
me in the night.
As the moon calls
out to the sleeping
sun into the distance?

Yet stars glaze above us
as a beacon of their love.

As morning comes,
darkness is pulled back
into the deepness of the void.

And the moon kisses the sun
good morning as the sun kisses
the moon goodnight.

Only to meet again
at the distance between
morning and goodnight.

COUNTING STARS

Looking into the night sky.
As stars guide us throughout
the night.

For morning breaks
at the sight of goodbye.

Thou our hearts forever counting
the stares of the night.

For in this moment
our hearts are forever
burning bright at the
taste of a kiss goodnight.

TOMORROW IS PROMISED

You looked at me
as our lips
said goodnight.

Yet words never formed phrase.
Only the touch of capture saliva
confirmed a forever lasting
promise that tomorrow
will bring.

I'll see you
later.
Goodnight.

Chapter Two

Everlasting Love

JOURNAL ENTRY "MONTH OF MAY."

I rushed straight home and grabbed my journal. I had to write every detail about tonight down, every detail about you, love. A maiden of the heavens, as the stars align around us tonight.

But in the glimpse of tonight my thoughts burns of you.

MORNING DESIRE

Stars align in the midnight sky
but only a kiss from you
consumes these lips.

My first love.
My first kiss.

For at the break of morning light
your face is the object of my desire
the object that consumes my thoughts.

EVERLASTING LOVE

Thy love is for everlasting
for thoughts of you crushes
like the morning tides.

For only the glimpse of your hair
flowing in the midnight sky
for love itself
she has bewitched me.

Yet I come willingly into her arms.
Not even Calliope could create
an epic poetry of the melody
thy love possess.

Nor Aphrodite herself could
compare to loves beauty.

For my heart is forever placed
like thorns on a single rose.

Bound by a single kiss goodnight.

MORNING BREAKS

Morning love breaks and here I lay
thinking of you.

Owe how last night was the best
night of my life.

Yet all I know is that I want to spend
every day with you.

JOURNAL ENTRY "MONTH OF MAY."

The phone ringed once, then twice, yet at the third ring I answer to an unknown caller that turned out to be you. Graduation was today, it was the end of tomorrow and the beginning of something new.

I thought to myself, how could I be captured in your eyes? How could I compare to other suitors, who are within your grasp? But I come willingly towards a journey unknown. Hello, I said answering the phone. "Do you want to meet up for graduation?" She asked. Yes! I will see you at there at 2 p.m. I replied.

SMALL THOUGHTS

Thoughts of you love
floods my mind with ease.

Thinking to myself
what should one wear
to empress thee.

Maybe a green tee dress shirt
and blue jeans.

That should do the trick
or maybe I'm over thinking it
or maybe I'm just missing your lips.

JOURNAL ENTRY "MONTH OF MAY."

Its 2pm, time to go. Seeing you in the hallway love, such a perfection of beauty as lips are pressed sealed, but here you stand waiting for me. You introduced me to your friends, jocks I would call them or maybe it's that I don't fit in, but I will follow your lead willingly.

Graduation ceremony seemed to took forever, but forever seems like a period of grace and peace within your presence. Someone called out your name, as we looked behind us and realized that it was your parents. By the look on your father face I could tell that I didn't have his approval. Although your mom came with accepting arms of love. But then you looked at me and asked me to ride with you to the graduation after party. Yes, I screamed inside, but nodded to your eyes.

THY LOVE IS LIKE SUMMER

Thy love is like summer
warm and temperate at every corner.
Blooms at the sight of May.
thou at times it may seem too sharp
to resist.
Often too hot to coexist.

Yet thy love is like summer
bound by eyes first sight
and lips first kiss.

JOURNAL ENTRY "MONTH OF MAY."

I stared at you the whole drive there, thinking about how one could make such a beautiful creature such as yourself. As always, your eyes caught me looking, as your checks formed a smile. Love, I am forever mesmerized in your presence as I am forever yours.

SUMMERTIME LOVING

Summer breaks at the love of May.
But if loving you is consequences
then promise to smother me
with your love at every chance.

Only to be ended
by a final kiss of summer.

SIGHT OF LOVE

They say falling in love
is a choice.

Then why does it feel
as if the laws of free will
doesn't apply at the sight
of you?

My heart forever tangle
within your reach.
and pulled at the
thought of you.

Yet I am forever
woven within the fabrics of your heaven.
As for love itself is written in the heavens
amongst the stars.

JOURNAL ENTRY "MONTH OF MAY."

We arrived at the graduation party that was hosted by your friends. Yes, parties are always nice when it is with you. We spent hours walking around meeting everyone and playing drinking games, it felt as if I could stay within this moment forever with you.

CATCH ME IF YOU DARE

Catch me if you dare
nine shots of tequila
to spare.

Three shots in
I confess my love
to you.

Six shots in
you said the feeling
is mutual too.

Nine shots in
we both hit
the dance floor.

As others lay waste
we dance the night away.
Eyes locked as lips
smother away.

Only to be captured
throughout the midnight gazes.

KISS ME INTO TONIGHT

Kiss me into tonight
hands against hands
as we dance throughout
the night.

Forever mesmerized within
each other's eyes.

As our lips dance
at the taste of moonlight.

JOURNAL ENTRY "MONTH OF MAY."

We dance the night away and kissed for hours. Shots after shots, round after round living in the midnight moment amongst the stars. But time itself seemed to have passed its curfew. You asked me to drive us back home, so I grab the car keys. Here we go driving into the midnight breeze.

It was an hour drive back to the city as I looked over as saw you fast asleep, for only the heavens itself could create such a thing. My head started to pound as I tried to remain focus on the road, but then I felt a taste of blood kiss my lips as my eyes started to close while driving into the midnight mist.

Boom! It's an accident. Love, we had an accident.

JOURNAL ENTRY "MONTH OF MAY."

We arrived at the hospital badly bruised. As for your car, it was totaled. Needles stuck throughout my arms, as I slowly came into conscious. Where are you love, are you ok? I looked over my shoulders and saw my parents face as tears slowly started to fade away. But then you walked into my room and asked, if I was ok.

Your father rushed in behind you with your mother trying to hold him back, as he threatens me to stay away from you. But who could blame him, for this is all my fault. I'm truly sorry love. The doctor came in the room baring bad news. As he looked at me and started to explain the reason for my blackout. I found myself felling as if the next words that come out of his mouth will be the beginning of the end. He said, "sir the reason that you fainted behind the wheel is because our test results shows that your cancer has returned." After a 6 yearlong battle, my cancer has return to take my life. No! How could this be I thought to myself, that a promise for forever could be faded by a single thing called cancer. I have cancer love.

WORDS OF OTHERS

Words of others
floods my mind.

Could this be it?
The final days at
the grasp of true
love kiss.

For love itself is eternal.
Yet here I lay slowly
fading away from
the reaches of your love
and the reaches of your kiss.

JOURNAL ENTRY "MONTH OF MAY."

The room felt into silence as a single word known as cancer came into existence. But how could this be? How could I be slowly fading into nonexistence at the break of finding true love. I watched as my parents felled to their knees, but you walked over to me and promised me that you would never leave my side. However, I asked you to go home and get some rest instead, but you insisted to stay. Please love, I said as your looked at me with teary eyes and said goodbye. I'll see you tomorrow.

I sat in the hospital room fighting thoughts that rambled in my mind, that the end was near.

COUNTING ROSE PEDDLES

Here I lay.
A thorn cut from
a single rose
tossed into the darkness
of tomorrow.
Just an emptiness void
of uncertainty.

Here I lay
counting rose peddles
as if winter itself
has overcame summers
bloom and peddles of love
fallen to waste.

Yet here I lay
counting rose peddles
until thy love fades away
at the endless counts
of my days.

DRIFTING INTO THE NIGHT

Drifting into the night
were darkness creeps
at your side.

For what once was
could never be
and what once was
meant to be
can never be seen.

For the void of emptiness
creeps at your side
and takes the place
that once were memories.

JOURNAL ENTRY "MONTH OF MAY."

Morning came like a thief in the night. But here you are at my side, as my eyes opens to my new life. Tell me love, are you here to stay? Because time itself is ticking away. One week pass and you are still here with me, one week lead into two weeks and two weeks lead into a month of you never leaving my side. Maybe this is love after all, I thought to myself.

Chapter Three

Lady Of The Sea

JOURNAL ENTRY "MONTH OF JUNE."

The month of June came baring gifts of love, as my cancer treatment started to bring in good news. I thought to myself, maybe life is not so bad after all. We decided to take a trip to the beach with your parents, although your dad still had his doubts. But as always, I'll follow your lead willingly. The drive was long, but we arrived at the beach in malibu.

DEEP BREATHS OF LIFE

What is life without love?
If not a needle in a haystack
just an endless nightmare
called loneliness.

WONDERING LOVE

Take me down by the sea
where water kneel at your feet
and eyes taste a sight of new life
as ears welcomes the whispers
of morning breeze.

LADY OF THE SEA

Owe lady of the sea
whose ocean eyes
sparkle at the sight
of morning light.

What have you done to me?
look how you have drawn
me towards your sea.

Owe lady of the sea
I am forever trapped
within your currents pull.
For other mermaids
may surround thee.

Yet these eyes are only
captured by your waters
and ears can only hear
your sirens song.

I am forever drawn to thee.
lady of the sea.

JOURNAL ENTRY "MONTH OF JUNE."

We soaked in the morning sun as I stared into your eyes, mesmerized by your beauty. As always you caught me looking and smiled back at me. "Do you think we should do a little sightseeing after the beach and maybe the two of us can grab dinner afterwards?" She said, looking at me with those ocean eyes. Sure, I replied. If only she knew that the only thing that mattered to me was being in her presence.

We spent hours soaking on the beach and playing in the sea, it felt as if we were the only two people that existed in the world and all my worries no longer existed. But the truth is, who knows how long I have or even if I could beat cancer again. I tried to remind myself to stay focus in the moments that I get to spend with you. Six hours had past by, when we finally decided that it was time to go and get food. Tacos! I want Tacos, she said as I watched her tie her hair into a ponytail. We arrived at a local taco shop and drunk margaritas for over an hour, while smashing eight tacos a piece. The day seemed young at every second we spent together, but then the phone ringed. My doctor was calling me, I thought to myself, he must be calling about good news. But as I answer the phone, I heard a shake in his voice as he insisted that we speak as soon as I make it back to Los Angeles California. I told him that I would come to his office once we made it back to the city.

It was four o'clock when we finally decided to tour around the city of malibu and ended our day with a final walk along the beach, as I watch you take down your hair and let it float in the wind. later we arrived back at the hotel after talking for hours on the beach about our future and college plans. Your father wanted you to attend Harvard as he did, but your dream was to study at NYU and live in New York City. Restless we both were as we arrived at our hotel room. You looked at me and started to kiss my cheeks as I held you throughout the night amongst the stars.

A CALL IN THE NIGHT

A call in the night
as arms fold at
your side and hands
curl around your thighs
drifting slowly into midnight.

A call in the night
tangle dancing within fabric
sheets as the heavens
gaze above us.
Forever captured by the
taste of one's lips
and the pleasures of
one's feast.

A call in the night
for lullabies sound off
throughout the night as
we become one within
the tangling scene of
midnight.

BEYOND THE NIGHT LIGHTS OF MIDNIGHT

Beyond the night lights of midnight
let our hearts forever shine bright
at a kiss to forever within
heavens eyes.

Until death herself close eyes and
reopen them to a new morning
light.

JOURNAL ENTRY "MONTH OF JUNE."

The midnight breezed brushed against my skin as I awoke from my sleep. But here you lay next to me fast asleep, as for your beauty is unmeasurable. My Journal! Where my journal? There it is, I must write this moment down as a night I never want to forget.

FOREVER BOUND

Thy love is forever
and so is mine.

Forever bound
yet written between these
lines of unspoken words.

Forever bound
by the love thee has for me
and the love I have for thee
blossoming between the tangling
scenes of midnight.

Forever bound
by the taste of pleasure
and the breath of the
midnight breeze floating
within the fabrics sheets
as I am forever bound to thee.

LOVE HEALS WITH TIME

They say time heals
but I'm still learning.

I'm still dreaming amongst
the heavens.
I'm still dreaming amongst
the stars.
But I'm glad that
I get to dream with you.

For even in the break
of morning light.
You are the object
that consume me and
the object that heals me.

You are my healing.

MORNING LIGHT

The night sky breaks away
at the sight of morning light.
Yet here I lay next to thee.

For morning calls out
to the welcoming of
a new day.

The welcoming of a new life
as eyes open to the sight
of another day of life
and lungs take in what
was once meant to be
tomorrow's breeze.

THY MORNING KISS

Thy morning kiss
compels my thoughts.
You are the object of my desire
and thy morning kiss is the pulse
that beats my heart.

Yet even in the distance of tomorrow
thy morning kiss seems
to never loses its pulse.
So even in death my heart
will beat for thee.

TOGETHER IN LOVE

Is this not love?
Is this not real?
Is this not meant to be?
For time will tell.

Sometimes stars
do fall out the sky.

Sometimes love
is no longer written
in heavens eyes.

But I come towards
your love willingly.
Willingly to fight
and willingly to
love and be
loved by you.

JOURNAL ENTRY "MONTH OF JUNE."

Morning came with butterflies as I watched you sleep peacefully, knowing that bad news was ahead of me once we arrive back home. I shucked your shoulder trying to awake you from your sleep, for it was time to check out of the hotel and head back home. The drive back home felt long as we sat in the back seat of your parents' car, I stayed silence the whole drive back home. I was wondering if bad news was ahead of me. the doctor wouldn't tell me much over the phone, but insisted that we speak in his office, so I guess love itself is like a flicker in the wind. It was about an hour or two when we arrived back to the city. Traffic in Los Angeles California is always the worse, but I enjoyed every moment I have with you, love.

TASTE OF LOVE

They say love is a drug.
Then I must have an addiction
because loving you is a reflection
of everything I was missing
before I met you.

For love
you carried me
in my time of need.

You fought for me
and stayed even when
time itself told you
to stay away.

You held those wombs
that were unforeseen.
You loved me.

Then if love is a drug.
Then I'll be first in line
to be subscribed
for a taste of thee.

COUNTING DAYS

Time flies
beyond heavens eyes
as fate seem to
be sealed away.

A long road
with a destination unknown
seem to have meet its end.

The clock ticks
once then twice
again, and again.

Slowly fading
to the sound
of counting days
until the end.

Chapter Four

Forbidden Love

JOURNAL ENTRY "MONTH OF JUNE."

3pm. It was 3pm., when we arrived at your house, your family home was one of the biggest houses I have ever seen and something that I could never afford. But I pray that my love will be enough for you. Your dad asked me to help him unpack the car, however I figured it was his way of asking me for a peptalk. I agreed and started to help him, but that's when he asked me about my future and suggested that I didn't hold you back from attending Harvard. Did he not know that Harvard wasn't your dream but his? I informed him that I would never hold you back from your dreams, love. He looked at me and said, "I'm glad we have this understanding." All I could do was smile as the words left his mouth. As we walked back to the house, I thought to myself that maybe you could attend your dream school in New York, and I could attend a local community college nearby. We could get an apartment and life could no-longer be a dream, but a reality.

Ring! Ring! My cell phone was sounding off, it was my doctor calling me. Hello, I said answering the phone nervously, "Are you back in the city?" he said. I informed him that I was back in the city, and I would be headlining to his office shortly after I finished unpacking. It was 5:50 pm., when I arrived at the hospital, hoping to receive good news regarding my cancer treatment. The doctor had a huge folder in his hand, as he asked me to sit in the empty chair. I was nervous, more than nervous but I remained calm as he start to go over my results and that's when he told me that my cancer had progressed and that I could have months or years to live. He suggested that I start a new treatment that was still under trial, I thought to myself, "what else did I have to lose other than love itself." I paused at the words that was coming out of his mouth, as he stated that there was no time frame regarding my situation. I walked out his office shaking and loss of words but all I knew was that I had to tell my parents. It was 7pm., when I made it home, as I sat my parents down and told them the news regarding my cancer result and treatment process, I watched tears come down their faces as all hope was lost. Yet, all I could think about was love. That night I couldn't sleep; I was thinking about all the ways I could tell you. Love, the thoughts of you floods my mind throughout the midnight sky.

DREAMFUL DREAMS

What is life
if not a dream?
Is life not a dream
of scenery with you?

Hair floating in the wind
as lips are sealed tight.

Is love not filled
with endless thoughts?

Is love not filled
with pleasures of lullabies
sounding off throughout
the midnight sky?

A dreamful dream
one could wish
that moments like
this could last
like a forever
kiss of love.

LOVING SUMMER

For this is love in summer.
Yet at the break of dawn
the season change.

But your love remains
forever captured within summer.

For flowers bloom
to welcome a new season.
Yet know that
thy love is with me
and mines is with thee.

FADING LOVE

Is this not to be?
Is this not love?
Is love not to be?

Slowly fading
from a glimpse
of a dream.

Yet I still
fight for thee.
To love
and be loved
by thee.

TAKE MY LOVE WITH YOU

Take my love with you.
Take my love when
I'm gone.
For time itself
has made its mark.

But I'll still love thee
beyond the lights
of heaven's eyes.

I'll love thee
until thy love
is once again with me.

JOURNAL ENTRY "MONTH OF JUNE."

Morning came and here I lay with missed calls from you. I sat in my room for hours thinking about what I was going to tell you, but how could I tell you that there was no cure to my cancer, how could I tell you that our love would be ended by time itself. I finally boost up the courage to come see you, as I grabbed my car keys and headed out the door. 10am. It was 10am, when I arrived outside of your house, not knowing that I was arriving to an argument between you and your dad. You guys were arguing over your decision to attend NYU and not Harvard. "It's all your fault!" He said as he looked at me with fire in his eyes as if it was the day that we first meet. We started to argue, while you and your mother tried to calm both of us down, but then the words slipped out of my mouth. "I'm dying!" "I'm dying!" I said, looking fearfully into his eyes as the room become a silent barrel. I informed your father that NYU was your dream and that he should be proud of you for following your heart even if its not with me.

We both looked at each other and apologies for our outburst, as you walked towards me and wrapped your arms around me. "We are in this together." She said, as if she was looking into my soul with those ocean eyes. The entire month of June was full of love and romance as we spent every second together, we started to travel around to different cities to knock off a couple things on our bucket list before it was time for you to attend college. Love itself seemed like a dream.

LOVES REFLECTION

What is love
if not a
reflection of you?

Calm and clear as the sea
Yet at times its waves
may capture thee
within its currents flow.

Yet if love is a reflection
then let it be a reflection
of you.

CLOUDY DREAMS

Cloudy dreams surrounds me
with the capture image of you.
For a forever love
seem to no longer exist.
Yet I willingly accept
the challenge to fight
for thee.

For thy love is my strength
and without it
I am weak.

For if my heart
is not loved
by thee.
lord let it beat
no more.

But if my heart
is loved
by thee.
Lord let it be
written amongst
the stars.

FORBIDDEN LOVE

So, if loving you is forbidden
then let me commit treason.
Because loving you
was everything I was missing
before I met you.

You see
The world will try
to tell you things
about love.
Yet none of those things
compares to you.

Nor can the definition
of love
compete against you.
Nor can Aphrodite herself
stand next to you.

So, if loving you is forbidden
then call me a forbidden lover.
Because nothing compares
to love and be loved by you.

PROMISE ME TOMORROW

Tomorrow comes
and I'm here.

You said you'll
be here in the morning
then promise me your
love will always be near.

Tomorrow comes
and I'm here.

Thinking about all the memories
and time we shared.
You said you'll
be here in the morning.
Then promise me
you'll kiss me then.

Promise me you'll
kiss me until the end.
Promise me tomorrow.

PICTURES ON THE WALL

Pictures on the wall
are slowly falling
as time ticks away.

Happy memories that once
stood tall are slowly
fading away.

Yet I know
that in heavens eyes
our love will be.

Until then
I'll wait for thee.

As pieces of glass fall.
Palms are bruised
by cuts of love
and memories
no longer hold waste.

Yet thy love
will forever
be captured
within a memory

of a midnight kiss
that will never
fade away.

FOREVER IN ARMS

Capture me
within your arms
so that my love
may bring thee comfort.

Capture me
within your arms
so that thee
may no longer
miss me.
But remember
that my love
will be a guide
for thee
and guide thee
back to me.

For our love
is written
in the heavens
amongst the stars.

Chapter Five

Time Flies

JOURNAL ENTRY "MONTH OF JULY."

The month of July seemed to have come flooding inn, as I continued cancer treatment trails trying to buy more time with you and out beat death itself. We spent the month of July picking out apartments for you in New York and started planning days that I would come visit between my treatments, once you had started college in late fall semester. Summer felt young and so were we. We spent every second together, slowly forgetting about what was ahead of us. Our parents started to host family dinner nights every Tuesday's and Thursday's, although I never would have thought that there would come a day that me and your dad would become so close, yet here we are friends at last. However, one thing remains and that's time itself.

BROKEN WORDS

Broken words
do not have meaning.
Broken words
do not have thoughts.

For they are broken
and broken they shall
be.

For they are words
not cuts
not bruises
not wombs
that can be healed.

Yet broken words
are words
and words
hold no meaning
over my soul.

Nor do they
control my heart.
For my heart
carries love
and love
heals all.

SHADES OF LOVE

Is your love not shades of color?
Is it not a representation
of my love for thee?

For all the shades it possess
one thing is certain
is that it has
capture me.

As my heart is forever
captured by thee
and with all the shades
thee possess
promise to cover me
with your love
and shade me
with your kiss.

NOTHING IS FORBIDDEN

Nothing is forbidden
Not even love itself.
Sometimes we must see
what is and not what is not.

Sometimes love is forbidden.
Sometimes love is written.
Sometimes it gazes amongst the stars
waiting to be capture in one's heart.

Yet nothing is forbidden
not even love itself.
Sometimes love is hidden.
Sometimes love is waiting
to be capture in one's eyes.
For at times love
can be restless
and captured
by a single kiss
within midnight.

JOURNAL ENTRY "MONTH OF AUGUST FINAL ENTRY."

The month of July was a blast, we travel almost the whole month as you dared me to do activities that I wouldn't normally do. But here we are in the months of August as summer comes to its end. My sickness was getting worst by the day, but you continued to help me find comfort within each second, we spent together, I could fill our time together was coming to an end and I knew that you felt it too, love.

Saturday August 17th was a Friday that I would never forget, I woke up unable to get out of bed. My voice was almost gone, but I managed to call out my parent's name. The end is near I fear, as my parents came rushing into my room seeing me almost paralyzed. My mom called the ambulance to come assist with taking me to the emergency room. I felt pain throughout my body as they stuck needles in me. This is the end, I thought to myself as I look up and saw you walking into the hospital room. "I'm here!" "I'm never leaving." She said, holding my hand as I drift into thought, while being under the influence of medication.

WHEN I'M GONE

When I'm gone
would you still be there
to love me amongst
the heavens eyes.

When I'm gone
would you blow me a kiss
and say your goodbyes
like spreading my ashes
across the sky
only to flow alone
amongst the lonely nights
wishing I was here
but knowing I'm gone
at first sight.

When I'm
would you be there
to kiss me goodbye.

REMEMBER ME

Remember me when I'm gone.
Remember me when you're all alone.
Like birds our memories fly south
as our love bloom north.

Remember me when I'm nothing more
but ashes left behind.
Remember my smile.
Remember my laugh.
Remember all the years I had.

Remember when I made you mad.
Remember when I made you sad.
Remember when we had long talks.
Remember how thy love buzzed
like honeybees at ever thought.

Remember me when I'm gone
souring in the night sky.
Remember me and all my goodbyes
not knowing that this would be
my last goodbye.

Promise me thy love will never die.
Remember me as you dream goodnight.
Remember me to the end of time.
Remember me for this is goodbye.

KISS FROM LADY OF THE NIGHT

Owe lady of the night
here I lay gently into the night
waiting for a final kiss goodnight
for father time has clocked out
for tonight.
Yet thy kiss consume multitudes
of thought rambling in my mind.

Ye pray thy kiss comes gently
and thy presence is tranquil.
Though it does not bring ye comfort
for certainty remains to be reviled.

She comes throughout the day and night
for time holds no bond at her sight.
Her kiss can be sharp
and painful at times.

Yet ye pray thy kiss comes gently
throughout the night
as for time has lost it tick
and words never form at her side.

Ye kneels at a kiss
from the lady
of the night.
A final kiss goodnight.

JOURNAL ENTRY "THE END."

It was 5am, when the last breath of life was drawn. Yet amongst the eyes of the heavens, I will forever watch over thee. I will watch you go into my room after I'm gone from this life and find my journal and read of our love. I will watch you start college in the late fall in New York and make new friends. I will watch you pick out your first apartment and hang up the pictures of our time together, and I will watch you cry because you miss me. But then you will remember my love for you and that I will always be with you. Love, I will watch you always, until we meet again amongst the heavens and the stars, because our love was written in the heavens amongst the stars.

LOVES CORE

Love is like the desert sands
it's warm and heavy
it flows in the air
it covers your heart
and sinks your soul.

The pain is pleasure
the rage is joy.
There's never enough
in which you'll
crave for more.

The passion of love
it will always make
you want more.

You can run or face it
the choice is yours
the deep dreams and
softness of loves pores
will have your soul
drowning in the sands
of the desert floor
with only you craving
for the darkness of
loves core.

Knowing there's always
a craving for more.

About The Author

Braodrick Patrick is an African American author and illustrator. He started writing poetry at a young age and dreamed of one day sharing his poetic thoughts with the world. Growing up in a small town in Mississippi, Braodrick grew up studying Shakespeare and was inspired by him as a poet, which he hopes to one day be. After high school he went to college at the University of Mississippi and studied business, where he received multiple degrees in, but his passion for poetry has never left his side. Throughout this collection he continues to explore a variety of themes and emotion that we as humans experience when being in love. Braodrick hopes to one day perform and share his poetry throughout the world.

www.ingramcontent.com/pod-product-compliance
Lightning Source LLC
Chambersburg PA
CBHW071732040426
42446CB00011B/2332